SPACE JUNK!

Contents

Waste in Space! — page 2

Kirk and the Space Vac — page 12

Simon Cheshire

Story illustrated by Chris Garbutt

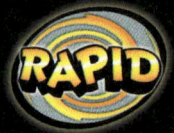 # Before Reading

Find out about

- The junk that floats around in Space

Tricky words

- Earth
- tiny
- paint
- float
- spacecraft
- damage
- astronaut
- glove

Introduce these tricky words and help the reader when they come across them later!

Text starter

There is a lot of junk on Earth but did you know that there is a lot of junk in Space too? Most of the junk in Space is tiny, but even tiny bits of junk can do damage.

Waste in Space!

There is a lot of junk on Earth, and there is a lot of junk in Space.

Some junk in Space is tiny.

Tiny bits of paint float around in Space.
If they hit a spacecraft, they could damage it.

A speck of paint made a hole in a space shuttle window.

Some junk in Space is big.

A spacecraft lost a hatch door. The door is floating around in Space!

An astronaut lost a glove.
The glove was floating around in Space for a year.

What happens to the junk?

Some junk burns up as it comes down to Earth, but some junk does not burn up.

Some junk could be floating in Space for 1000 years.

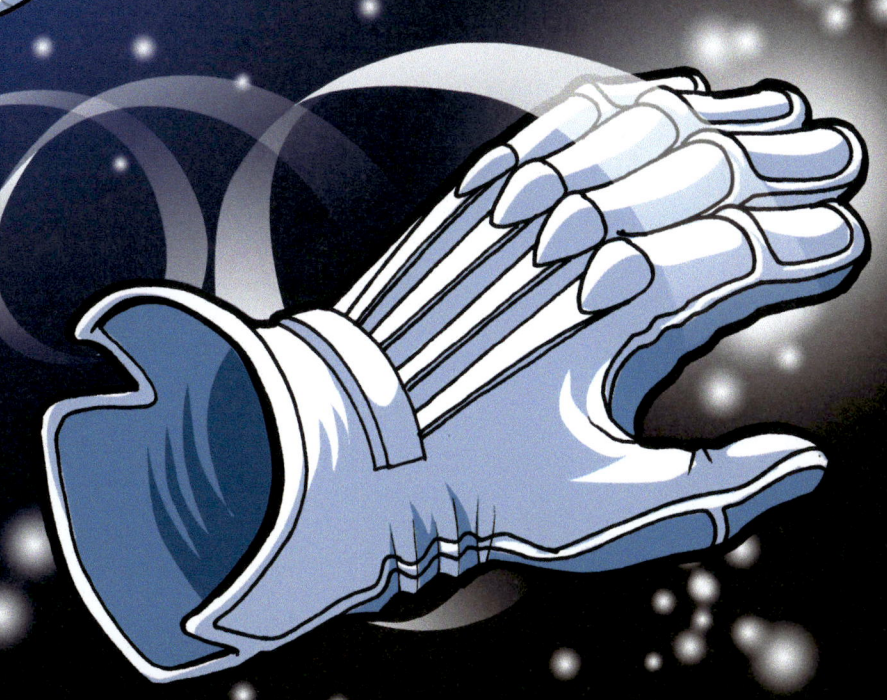

Could junk land on you?
Some junk does come down to Earth.

There are 110,000 things floating in Space.

Some junk lands in the sea but some junk lands on Earth. You could be hit on the head!

Keeping safe

You could look up to see if some Space junk is coming down to Earth.

Or . . . you could wear a hard hat!

Quiz

Text Detective

- Why is Space junk dangerous?
- What is the most amazing fact you have learned about Space junk?

Word Detective

- **Phonic Focus:** Initial consonant clusters

  Page 3: Sound out the four phonemes in 'Space'. Can you blend the first two sounds?
- Page 4: Find a word made from two smaller words.
- Page 7: Can you find the word 'some' three times?

Super Speller

Read these words:

there   year   head

Now try to spell them!

HA! HA! HA!

Q Did you hear about the man who thought he was a dustbin?

A He kept talking rubbish!

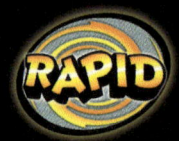

Before Reading

In this story

 Kirk, a Space Cop    Joe, a Space Cadet

 Zorgon, their enemy

Introduce these tricky words and help the reader when they come across them later!

Tricky words

- Space Base
- Space Vac
- waste
- radar
- something
- turned
- wait
- blown

Story starter

Commander Kirk is a Space Cop travelling across Space in his starship. Joe, a Space Cadet, is on board too. Kirk and Joe battle against their evil enemy, Zorgon. Space Base has just sent Kirk their latest invention – a Space Vac that could suck up waste in Space!

Kirk and the Space Vac

Space Base gave Kirk a Space Vac. The Space Vac could suck up waste in Space.

Joe looked at the radar. "Sir," said Joe, "there is something on the radar."

Kirk looked at the radar. "It is Zorgon," he said, "and the Big Blob."

"I must do something," said Kirk. "The Big Blob will eat us up!"

"Sir," said Joe, "I have a plan. I will suck up the Big Blob with the Space Vac."

Joe turned on the Space Vac but he pressed **BLOW**, not **SUCK**.

"You turned the Space Vac to **BLOW**," said Kirk.

"Sorry, sir," said Joe.

The Space Vac blew Zorgon into the Big Blob.

The Big Blob began to eat Zorgon.

But the Big Blob did not eat Zorgon. It spat him out.

The Space Vac blew and blew. It blew Zorgon and the Big Blob into Space.

"Just you wait," said Zorgon. "I will be back!"

Quiz

Text Detective

- What did the Big Blob do to Zorgon?
- Do you think Joe is a good Space Cadet?

Word Detective

- **Phonic Focus:** Initial consonant clusters

  Page 20: Sound out the four phonemes in 'spat'. Can you blend the first two sounds?
- Page 15: Find a word made up of two smaller words.
- Page 19: Find a word meaning 'started'.

Super Speller

Read these words:

turned   sorry   wait

Now try to spell them!

HA! HA! HA!

Q What do you call a crazy astronaut?

A An astro-nut!